the Conversation

the Conversation

AN INTIMATE JOURNAL OF

THE EMMAUS ENCOUNTER

JUDY SALISBURY

15   14 13 12 11   6 5 4 3 2 1

Library of Congress Control Number: 2011921442

ISBN 978-1-936716-17-3

Printed in the United States of America

Copyright © 2011 by Judy Salisbury

Published by
Lederer Books
A division of
Messianic Jewish Publishers
6120 Day Long Lane
Clarksville, Maryland 21029

Distributed by
Messianic Jewish Resources Int'l.
www.messianicjewish.net
Individual and Trade Order line: (800) 410-7367
Email: lederer@messianicjewish.net

ENDORSEMENTS

"*The Conversation* brings to life that famous encounter between the two disciples and our Lord Yeshua on the road to Emmaus. While it is based in part on an imaginative reconstruction, it is filled with the throbbing pulse of the excitement of the sensational impact that our Lord's resurrection should have on all of our lives."

Dr. Walter C. Kaiser, Jr.
President Emeritus
Gordon-Conwell Theological Seminary

"This little book does a big thing. It takes the age-old truths of the prophetic accuracy of the Bible and communicates it in an appealing literary format. In so doing, it portrays one of the great apologetic tools of the Christian faith in an engaging and readable form."

Dr. Norman Geisler
Distinguished Professor of Apologetics
Veritas Evangelical Seminary

"I found *The Conversation* remarkable and riveting. Judy Salisbury portrays Yeshua in such a beautiful, gentle, perfect way. Tears were rolling down my face as I envisioned him through her words. She did a fantastic job with the Scriptures, networking them all together with profound significance—the mark of a seasoned apologist. The book, as a whole, is fascinating, captivating, eye-opening, and doctrinally sound. I also think it would make an awesome movie. The Lord's hand was definitely in this project. I can't wait for my Jewish friends to read it!"

Jennifer Sands
International Christian Speaker
Author and 9/11 Widow

"An interesting story, though fictional, yet *The Conversation* rings with possibility. I pray that it will have a wide reading and that many will come to believe that Yeshua is the Messiah of Israel!"

Dr. David Hocking
Founder, Hope for Today

"*The Conversation* is the most concise explanation of the Old Covenant foretelling Yeshua that I've ever read. It's brilliant. I love it. In fact the buildup was great and when I got to the why, I couldn't put it down."

Joan Phillips
Writer/Editor, The Christian and Missionary Alliance

"*The Conversation* is an excellent sketch of the sort of things that might have been said by Yeshua and the two on the way to Emmaus after the Resurrection. It presents a good number of the prophetic passages that we have reason to believe were recognized as Messianic in the early church. It gives us a good feel for how Cleopas and his friend might have reacted to these things as 'their hearts burned within them.'"

Dr. Robert C. Newman
Professor of New Testament
Biblical Theological Seminary
Director, Interdisciplinary Biblical Research Institute

"I was attracted to the subject matter of *The Conversation*, the two men, plus "the Stranger," on the road to Emmaus. I'm a visual person, and Judy Salisbury vividly paints the picture of prophecies regarding Messiah's suffering, death, and resurrection—and the purpose of it all—with flawless brushstrokes of color and accuracy. As I journeyed in my mind with these three I found myself also reflecting back to a trip my husband and I took to Israel. I wish I had had this powerful book to give to our Jewish guide. Prayerfully, he would understand that this account is not simply 'according to tradition,' as he stressed, but according to prophetic truth."

Jane Davis
Founder, President & Designer
Not So Plain Jane, Inc.
Tidings Of Love, Inc.

"Judy Salisbury has a way, like no other, to take us back in time on the road to Emmaus. Through *The Conversation* she beautifully and creatively unfolds an extraordinary dialogue that brings out scriptural insights, and spiritual progression. *The Conversation* can't help but change hearts. *A must read for all.*"

Donna Morley
Author, Conference Speaker
Co-founder, Faith and Reason Forum

Lovingly dedicated to
Brother Clarence Marvin Nagel
July 2, 1906 – July 6, 2008

Clarence's life will always exemplify for me
what true zeal for God really means.
Although I deeply miss "my oldest,"
I'm comforted knowing he now glories in
God's presence.
"Forever with the LORD. Amen!"

Contents

Acknowledgments

I would first like to express my thanks and appreciation to those who kindly took the time to review this work, to those who proposed suggestions, and especially to those who offered endorsements. I am honored and humbled by your kind words.

Special thanks to everyone at Messianic Jewish Publishers for making this work a reality and for all your hard work in putting together the finished product. Thanks also to Rabbi Barry Rubin for his insight and his tender heart for the Jewish People and to Lisa Donovan for her vision for this work.

Very special thanks to my dear friend, Joan Phillips, for her meticulous editing of the manuscript. You are such a blessing to me. No words can fully express my gratitude for your most excellent gift. Thank you, Elisa Laird, for the finishing touches.

My heartfelt thanks to Dennis and Lola Crawford for their wonderful suggestions to the original manuscript and for Lola's excellent counsel in her review of the final product. Their love, passion for the Lord, and generosity of fellowship are beyond words. Lola, it's so great to have you as my spiritual mom!

To my pastor and co-laborer in Yeshua, Denny Martinez—God bless you for your great encouragement through the years and for understanding my calling much better than many. Thank you for your support on various levels and for preaching God's Word so thoroughly and faithfully.

Deepest thanks to my husband, Jeff. For twenty–two years, you have been my lover and best friend. Without your constant love and support, the joy you bring to my life, and the green light to pursue my calling, this work would not be possible.

Affectionate thanks to my children, Nicole and Mikael. You are an absolute joy to me. I pray this work is a continual reminder to you of the power of God, who uses us in spite of our many flaws. Thank you for being such wonderful cheerleaders!

ACKNOWLEDGMENTS

Thank you, Abba Father, for condescending to use a broken, leaky vessel like me. Thank you that your Word is so powerful and your prophecies are so true. Thank you for granting me the gifts and wisdom to write this work, which I truly felt was beyond my ability. Thank you for sending your Son, the crowning glory of this work, to save me from my sins and myself and then making it possible for me to serve you with all my heart, soul, and mind. May you receive any honor and glory that might come out of this work, which I offer up as a sweet sacrifice of praise. You are worthy!

PREFACE–
How This Book Came to Be

Then beginning with Moses and with all the prophets,
he explained to them the things concerning
himself in all the Scriptures.
Luke 24:27

One verse that's all it was. Yet it sparked my soul and imagination. It was simply one small verse but one that is weighty with implication. In all the times I've read Luke 24:27, I cannot even begin to explain why it had never before impacted me as much as it did that cold January morning.

It was during my early Bible reading and prayer time. The sunlight had yet to penetrate the darkness outside my office window as I read through Luke's Gospel. Tears filled my eyes as I pondered aloud what it could have been like for those two downcast individuals who only felt sorrow and confusion over their recently crucified rabbi, beloved friend, and presumed coming king, Yeshua of Nazareth.

Why? I wondered, *Why couldn't we just have a little booklet insert to know what that conversation was like when those two men met that stranger on the road to Emmaus? What was it like? What did they feel? Oh, how I wish I had something that would take me there, to that road, to hear the impassioned exchange that must have taken place.*

Then it happened. Suddenly an overwhelming weight fell upon me, prompting me—no compelling me—to answer this task, which, I must confess, even the thought overwhelmed me. Feeling completely inadequate—not wanting to create something that might be a stumbling block for some, realizing that it would have to be a fictional account, and not wanting a lightning bolt to strike me between the eyes—I tried to put the notion out of my mind.

Yet my mind could not release the thought, nor the weight upon my heart to answer the call to this task, and by the end of the evening, I had been provided with enough confirmation that I knew I was indeed supposed to create this captivating little resource.

What you have in your hands is a book based upon one verse. It is an expanded version of Luke 24:27 from the very intimate perspective of the unnamed *talmid* (disciple). Working on this project was emotional and tedious but extremely rewarding to my heart, soul, and mind. My prayer is that you will be rewarded in like manner and that this resource will help you to grow in your confidence in the Scriptures, the fact of the Resurrection, and in faith in the Messiah.

If you are reading this book as a skeptic, you are searching for answers, or someone is *making* you read this, I am thrilled you are taking the time to do just that. My prayer for you is that you will fully consider the evidence contained herein and that you will follow that evidence through to its logical conclusion. After all, one of the main characters, Cleopas, is a skeptic, perhaps just like you. I pray with all my heart that whatever side of the fence you happen to be on, you will be blessed in your quest!

Your servant in Yeshua,
Judy Salisbury

The Encounter

"Do not let your heart be troubled; believe in God, believe also in Me."[1] I can hear his tender, confident words so clearly in my mind. I want so desperately to believe them, yet I must confess my heart is troubled; to the depth of my being I am troubled. Utter dismay and despair reigns in my heart. Could I have misunderstood his words, his life, and his works? Yeshua has died, and my hope has died with him. Now it is the third day and the horror of it all has become my reality.

A festival, by definition, is supposed to be festive. For the past few years it was, while he was with us. However, as I attended the waving of the omer in the Temple and the presentation of the first fruits with our people early this morning, I knew I was only going through the

1

motions. It amazed me how the priests were still able to fulfill what was necessary for this small festival—the preparation of the loaves through the evening and the sacrifice of the year-old lamb without defect as a burnt offering—in spite of the horrific events.[2]

My attention, at this point, has turned to going back home. The barley harvest was a good excuse to be on my way and staying seemed only to increase my stinging pain. I would return next week for the last day of the Feast of Unleavened Bread and not return again until the fiftieth day when the Counting of the Omer was complete, for *Shavuot* (Pentecost)—in celebration of the day the *Torah* was given to our people by Moses. I certainly had no desire to return to Jerusalem until then.[3]

During the next fifty days, when the barley is harvested, we would be wholly focused on all that God has done for his people. The Counting of the Omer is such a deep, intimate time of reflection, yet my mind feels clouded and confused.

To say that our return to our home village of Emmaus would feel like the longest two-hour trek we would ever journey would be an enormous understatement. Going back, feeling so empty and defeated and so confused and sorrowful when we had been so hopeful, seemed like walking into a dark cloud that could quite possibly suffocate us upon arrival. Indeed, going back for the barley harvest was a satisfactory reason, but we also realized that to stay could have even been dangerous in light of the distressing recent events in Jerusalem. My dear friend, Cleopas, solemnly consented to accompany me.

We, Cleopas and I, shared a common bond in our belief that Yeshua was perhaps the long-awaited one who would liberate Israel. But again, only confusion and, dare I say, fear grips our being.

There was a long silence between us as we passed through the large stone gate at an entrance to the city of Jerusalem. The city gate was usually abuzz with elders arguing some case or another, merchants occupying themselves with various business transactions, and blind or lame beggars calling out for mercy. Yet on this day, the mood seemed quite subdued as we ambled passed the lulled activity, which only punctuated our own somber mood.

"Now I know why it is our law that we do not rely on women for testimony," Cleopas stated. "Surely it must have been their grief that made them see this incredible vision of angels in his tomb this morning instead of his body."

"But Cleopas," I posed gingerly, trying not to invoke any more agitation, "Peter and John came to the tomb and also claimed that Yeshua's body was not there."

"Perhaps they happened upon the wrong tomb," Cleopas reasoned. It was almost as if he could console himself if he offered some type of rational explanation.

"But," I reminded, "his tomb was well known and well guarded. I cannot explain this either, but their passion has convinced me they must have seen something... or nothing. Well, something in light of the angels and nothing in light of his body."

"There are many things that can provoke one to..." Suddenly, Cleopas's expression changed as he stopped his reasoning mid-sentence. He stretched his neck forward to look past my left shoulder as he walked beside me to my right. I turned my head away from Cleopas and looked to my left. A man we did not recognize was walking along with us! Cleopas and I curiously glanced at each other, thinking it odd this man would simply stroll beside us as though he were just another traveling companion. I thought it quite peculiar that he should impose in this manner as we reasoned over these events; it was quite obvious he was able to hear us converse.

Puzzled, Cleopas and I just stared at the man, who simply looked nonchalantly straight ahead as the three of us walked side by side a bit further. We could not distinguish from his rather common attire what region he was from. His cloak, or mantle, was much like ours, white and woolen with the four prescribed tassels, the *tzitziot*, at the corners. Like us, his tunic fitted him closely about his neck, the sleeves were short, and the longer sleeves from his linen shirt underneath fell upon the tops of his hands as they casually swayed at his sides. The linen girdle wrapped, as ours, several times about his waist; his leather sandals were well worn.

The stranger was an ordinary-looking Jewish man. There was nothing distinct about his appearance that one would look at him and say, "Now there's a strapping King Saul."[4] I imagine that he would have blended in a crowd quite nicely.[5]

He carried no pack; no one else accompanied him, and we barely heard him approach. Still looking forward as if to see the end of his destination, the stranger casually asked, "What are you talking about with each other as you walk along?"[6]

Stunned, Cleopas and I stopped short in our tracks, amazed that anyone could imagine we would be speaking of anything other than the obvious. White dust from the rocky road billowed about our feet as we hung our heads at the thought of having to once again recount the awful circumstances that left our hearts so downcast. I, for one, could not speak. I felt a lump in my throat so large that I could hardly swallow. I took a deep breath and lifted my head back to contain the tears I felt welling up as if they would return to their place as they pooled in my eyes.

Cleopas, always so much bolder than I, lifted his head and answered almost sarcastically as though he needed to release the pain in his heart, "Are you the only person staying in Jerusalem that doesn't know the things that have been going on there the last few days?"[7]

The stranger looked back toward us from his position in the middle of the road and with as much innocence as a curious child to his mother, he asked simply, "What things?"[8]

We looked at the man with our mouths agape. We searched his expression for some speck of sarcasm in that we could not believe there could be *anyone* left in Jerusalem who did not know the events surrounding Yeshua. Yet his face held no mocking expression. He appeared to be sincerely curious. It seemed as if he honestly did not know about whom or what we were talking.

Cleopas slowly walked toward the man. I wasn't sure what he would say or if he concluded the same as I did regarding the innocence in the tone of the man's question. Cleopas began his impassioned explanation, "About Yeshua of Nazareth, who was a prophet, mighty in work and word before God and all the people," he was quite animated now, stepping closer to the eavesdropper as he continued, "and how our chief priests and rulers handed him over to be sentenced to death, to be crucified by the Gentiles as a criminal." Cleopas walked a few feet past him, gazing down the long road ahead and then painfully confessed, "But we were hoping that it was he who would redeem and set Israel free. Indeed, and besides all this, it is now the third day since these things occurred."

After a long silence from Cleopas, the man slowly turned his head and looked back down the road toward me with an expression as if prompting me to finish the story. I don't know why I felt suddenly nervous, but I also felt I had to address what he might have overheard even though I knew he might think I was absurd. "And, and," I approached him fumbling rather nervously yet unconsciously with a *tzitzit*, a fringe, from a corner of my mantle as I spoke, "moreover, some women of our company astonished us. They were at the tomb early in the morning but did not find his body."

I waited for the stranger's expression to change to some sort of disbelief, but his face looked as if to say, "Go on...," so I did. "And they returned saying that they had even seen a vision of angels, who said that, that..." I hesitated as the excitement in my mind caught up with the words from my mouth as I blurted, "that he was alive!"

His expression still did not change. It was almost a peaceful confidence if there is such a thing. I looked at Cleopas who rolled his eyes at me and then gestured with his hand as if to say, "You have gone this far you might as well tell him the rest." And I did! "So some of those who were with us went to the tomb, and they found it just as the women had said. But him," I felt my voice trailing off, "they did not see."9

A smile crossed the man's peaceful face. He strolled to where I stood on the road, put one hand upon my shoulder, and then guided me ahead to where Cleopas stood. He then placed his other hand upon Cleopas's shoulder as we now walked with the stranger between us. He gently shook his head as he said, "O foolish men and slow of heart to believe in all that the prophets have spoken!" Cleopas and I glanced across to each other behind his back. I guess we knew we should have been offended, but quite frankly, given the gentle way he said it, I felt graciously rebuked instead of insulted. Something in me told me he was right. Then, with authority, he posed, "Was it not necessary for the Messiah to suffer these things and to enter into his glory?"[10]

"The Messiah!" Cleopas shouted.

"Yes, the Messiah," the man stated confidently.

"But we know Messiah will be King! He will save our people. Yet if Yeshua was Messiah, why did he not liberate us from this oppressive rule our people endure?" Shaking his head, Cleopas added indignantly, "I've, I've never thought myself slow to believe the prophets!"

I tried to calm Cleopas by interjecting, "Perhaps, Cleopas, the gentleman means we are slow to *understand?*" I coyly smiled as I nodded encouragingly.

Cleopas, without acknowledging that I had said anything, continued, "I do believe what Yeshua told us when he was here. I loved him, believed him… love him… but now he's gone, literally gone, and what am I to think?"

I could no longer look Cleopas in the eye. It was as if he were revealing my heart before our unexpected, eavesdropping traveling companion. Once again, I felt that boulder in my throat.

"Come now," the man said with a smile on his face and utter compassion for our pain in his voice, "and let us reason together concerning these things."[11]

The Messiah Would Be King

We, the three of us now, walked heading toward Emmaus in the mid-afternoon sun through this rather rocky region. Our new traveling companion spoke with an understanding yet determined tone, "I can see in your eyes and hear in your voices that your hearts are clearly broken over the events surrounding this man you obviously love, but indeed Moses and the prophets spoke of these things. They spoke of Messiah's coming, his great miracles, and they did indeed, Cleopas, speak of his kingdom without end. But Moses and the prophets also spoke of his suffering, of him being the final atoning sacrifice necessary for the sin of the world."

"*Necessary* what he suffered? And what of his suffering... a suffering Messiah? I don't see it; I just don't see it." Cleopas responded in clear frustration. He reminded, "Our Yeshua was crucified as a criminal, and now his body is gone. What proof do we have, what hope do we have that what you say is true? Show me what I cannot grasp given that you seem so confident in your counsel. How can I know this man we believed to be the One is the one true Messiah? Satisfy my heart with some sort of answer. Satisfy my mind with proof that what you say is true, and I will not be so 'slow of heart' as you accuse."

Now the stranger was the one to stop abruptly on the dusty road as he looked directly into Cleopas's eyes while he said, unflinchingly, "Very well, because you seek an explanation and proof for what you cannot see plainly, I will help you see through what you've already witnessed with this Yeshua, whom you mourn, and the one prophesied."

I gasped. There was no argument from Cleopas now; his eyes were wide as he looked at the man. Something instinctive, intuitive, made us feel as if it were folly to question his wisdom, his knowledge, or his authority, as if somehow in some way what he shared would be from some kind of intimate knowledge of his own private access.

It was almost too much for my mind to grasp after so much confusion to suddenly feel as if I were now on the road to *enlightenment* instead of Emmaus. I felt this man was destined for this road at this moment to help us understand. I cannot explain how I knew I could so fully trust whatever explanation he offered.

I felt my heart pounding; my face felt hot and clammy, and no, it was not the afternoon sun that did it. I felt a fearful excitement. As odd as it sounds, I knew that I would know.

I felt as if he could not speak fast enough, yet his tone was calm and reassuring. Suddenly I wished this trip to be two days instead of two hours because I knew the longer we would stay with this man, the more we would learn from him.

Cleopas stepped closer to the man. As we faced each other, standing now in the middle of the road, he paused as if to calm himself. Then Cleopas said, "The Scriptures say Messiah would be king. You cannot deny we were expecting a king."

With that, my mind returned to just a week prior. We were not the only ones expecting a king to quash Roman rule. I thought back to the crowds, the excitement, the cries of, "*Blessed is the King who is coming in the name* of *ADONAI!*" and, "*Shalom in heaven!*" and, "*Glory in the highest places!*"[12] But one has to admit, he was seated on a young donkey, not a large white horse with flowing robes as a king would.

We hailed him as king, but he came seated as a servant. That had been curious to me. But now, as the man suggests, if we apply the events we witnessed, which our fathers before us foretold, then I am forced to realize the words of the prophet Zechariah, "*Rejoice greatly, O daughter of Zion! Shout in triumph, O daughter of Jerusalem! Behold, your king is coming to you; he is just and endowed with salvation, humble, and mounted on a donkey, even on a colt, the foal of a donkey.*"[13] "*Endowed with salvation,*" this stranger had my full attention.

"This man you loved was a humble man?" Our new traveling companion asked as he looked directly into my eyes. It was as if he were reading my thoughts regarding Yeshua's rather humble entry into Jerusalem.

"Oh, oh, yes, very humble." I thought back for a moment and then shared, "In fact, one of the twelve told us that the night before he… his…," I could not bring myself to say it, "Well, the night before, that he got up from the Passover meal, laid aside his garments, and taking a towel, he girded himself. Then he poured water into the basin and began to wash the *talmidim*'s feet and to wipe them with the towel with which he was girded.[14] He explained to them, you see, that he did this to offer an example of our service to each other, of what attitude we should have no matter how the LORD may use us. No matter how exalted our position, we are to serve humbly as he served."

"Indeed, he was humble," Cleopas added, "to the point of entering Jerusalem on a lowly donkey's colt."

Catching my gaze again, the man added with a slight grin, "As Zechariah said he would."

"Y-y-yes," I stammered, feeling as if I now had confirmation that he *was* reading my mind. Once again, he placed himself between us and then gestured that we continue walking.

"Yes, I do know the Scriptures," Cleopas said to himself aloud as he nodded. "I know God spoke to King David through the prophet Nathan saying, 'When your days are complete and you lie down with your fathers, I will raise up your descendant after you, who will come forth from you, and I will establish his kingdom. He shall build a house for my name, and I will establish the throne of his kingdom forever.'"[15]

Then, speaking rather passionately and directly to the stranger, he added, "There was a reason why we felt certain our coming king would deal with Rome once and for all. God, speaking through the prophet, told King David, 'I will also appoint a place for my people Israel and will plant them, that they may live in their own place and not be disturbed again, nor will the wicked afflict them any more as formerly, even from the day that I commanded judges to be over my people Israel; and I will give you rest from all your enemies.'"[16]

Cleopas then angrily muttered to himself, "One day he is hailed as the king we knew him to be; a week later he is betrayed by one of his own with the cries of 'Crucify him! Crucify him!' by the same crowd!"

The man nodded in agreement and then said, "Yes, a king was anticipated by all as Moses wrote, 'The scepter will not depart from Judah, or the ruler's staff from between his feet, until he comes to whom it belongs and the obedience of the nations is his.'[17]

"Also, Isaiah the prophet said, 'For a child will be born to us, a son will be given to us; and the government will rest on his shoulders; and his name will be called Wonderful Counselor, Mighty God, Eternal Father, Prince of Peace.'[18] In light of this, my friends, is it not obvious that a king can have various missions at various times and especially on foreign soil?"

Cleopas thought for a long moment. The silence was a bit uncomfortable as we walked along. I knew the answer. We both knew the answer to the man's question. But why was admitting the possibility so hard for us? Cleopas stroked his long beard as if hoping each time he'd grasp the dense whiskers some clever response would emerge in his mind. Yet only one could.

"True," came Cleopas's soft reply, "true."

Admitting that kings can serve as warriors as well as peacemakers or reconcilers made us begin to wonder if we could have indeed missed something more.

"Of Messiah's coming, Moses also wrote that ADONAI, God, as he cursed the serpent after Adam and Eve fell into sin, said, 'I will put enmity, between you and the woman, and between your seed and her seed; he will crush your head, and you will strike his heel.'[19] Isn't it obvious, my friends, that the crushing of Satan does not come without the striking of the one prophesied? Do you see that?"

We both nodded in unison, almost afraid to pose any more arguments contrary to the direction he seemed to be taking us. Was there a purpose in his suffering? We knew at this point that we had a lot to learn.

The Messiah Would
Be Rejected and Betrayed

As we continued our journey, the man then gently suggested, "I know, although it is difficult, we must discuss the various ways in which the Expected One was to suffer."

Cleopas and I sighed heavily as we glanced over to one another. The man paused for a moment then said, "Indeed the Scriptures state that he would be rejected by his people. You mentioned, Cleopas, a betrayal, specifically the betrayal from one of his own I believe and eventually by the crowds? You also mentioned the chief priests and religious rulers turning him over to be crucified?"

"Yes, yes." Cleopas said edgily, confirming the man's inquiry.

"But did not David write, 'Even my close friend in whom I trusted, who ate my bread, has lifted up his heel against me'?[20] And of what price did the betrayer receive for his deed?"

There was a bit of a grimace upon Cleopas's face as he slowly turned his head away. Judas was always a bitter subject for Cleopas, especially since he was fully aware of Judas's pilfering from the money bag. Because of his uneasy countenance I quickly interjected, "For thirty pieces of silver from the chief priests and elders."

"Quite right, again, as Zechariah foretold. And what was done with that silver? Surely the betrayer did not keep it," he stated confidently.

I glanced once more to Cleopas who was still looking off to the side, as if in his own world. I then said, "No, he did not. Judas Iscariot, remorseful for what he had done, knowing he had betrayed an innocent man threw the thirty pieces of silver into the Temple sanctuary to the chief priests and elders, who then…"

"… purchased a potter's field as a burial place for strangers,"[21] our informed traveling companion interrupted, finishing my sentence. "As Zechariah the prophet spoke, 'I said to them, "If it is good in your sight, give me my wages; but if not, never mind!" So they

20

weighed out thirty shekels of silver as my wages. Then the LORD said to me, "Throw it to the potter, that magnificent price at which I was valued by them." So I took the thirty shekels of silver and threw them to the potter in the house of the LORD.'²² And of Judas's remorse?" he asked.

This time Cleopas was quick to respond, yet his tone was quite solemn. "Judas went away and hanged himself." Although Cleopas was never pleased with Judas, knowing what kind of man he was, he also felt in his heart that had Judas repented for his betrayal as Peter did for denying Yeshua three times, surely he would have been forgiven.

Cleopas then sharply observed, "They purchased a potter's field. Yes, many of the chief priests and elders were so concerned for what was appropriate under the Law so as not to defile the Temple treasury regarding Judas's blood money, yet they were perfectly fine with violating a myriad of our other Jewish laws in order to hand over an innocent man to the Gentiles for crucifixion!"

I must confess, with this topic, I now felt quite uncomfortable. This was not something I wanted to think about, let alone discuss. Cleopas, of course, was referring to the horrendous mock trial Yeshua underwent. From start to finish it was an outrage of justice, judicial murder—pure and not so simple.[23] His arrest was illegal because it took place at night and through the agency of a traitor. The private examination before Caiaphas was illegal because it was also conducted at night.

The trial before the Sanhedrin also was totally illegal because the location of the trial was illegal and again conducted at night. Yeshua also had no defense. Caiaphas presented the charge instead of the leading witnesses. False witnesses were brought in for testimony although no two of them could even agree. It was an outrage! I hate to have to think of it—how Yeshua was told to confess, how the High Priest voted first by rending his robe, and then immediately declaring Yeshua deserved death. Yet, our beloved Yeshua was not guilty of the capital offense of blasphemy because he never pronounced the name of God, which could only be uttered once a year in the sanctuary of the Temple by the High Priest.

Beside all this, Pontius Pilate found no fault in him, and Herod sent him back to Pilate, essentially acquitting Yeshua as well. Oh, our Yeshua should have been freed. *He should have been freed!* Surely, he should not have been scourged let alone delivered up to be crucified.

So here we are, here I am, thinking back on these things and wondering if I could ever understand the *whys* of so many painful events in such a short amount of time. I so desperately wanted to believe this man could offer answers for these things. It seemed like so much, yet he did seem to pull the Scriptures together like a great mosaic.

I am tempted, with my thoughts turned to the trial, to offer some words from the Scriptures that come to my own mind. "Do not deliver me over to the desire of my adversaries, for false witnesses have risen against me, and such as breathe out violence. Do not let those who are wrongfully my enemies rejoice over me; nor let those who hate me without cause wink maliciously. For they do not speak peace, but they devise deceitful words... They opened their mouth wide against me; they said, 'Aha, aha, our eyes have seen it!'"24

When I think of Yeshua, so silent before the chief priests and the elders as he was accused and questioned, my mind quickly recalls our prophet Isaiah's words, "He was oppressed and he was afflicted, yet he did not open his mouth; like a lamb that is led to slaughter, and like a sheep that is silent before its shearers, so he did not open his mouth."25

However, rather than offering these passages as we traveled along, I knew what I really needed to do. I needed to focus and to pay attention, close attention. I needed to make sure that, as a veil is lifted, my eyes would see correctly and not simply what I *wanted* to see. But the Scriptures do seem to fit perfectly with what we witnessed. Some things cannot be concocted. Even so, as one lives through horrific events as what we witnessed, one's mind is generally not thinking, *Yes, of course, this is how it was foretold!* No, the last thing I wanted to do was to force any Scriptures into the situation in an attempt to tie them together.

As I look over at Cleopas, I am certain he felt the same. I must say that I was glad he expressed his concerns—yes, doubts—so openly before the man. It was amazing to me how very patient he was with my friend. He seemed to understand Cleopas's abrupt attitude, his questioning, his doubts, and his fears. Indeed, this stranger seemed to be a man of understanding on several counts.

The man then clarified, "So as foretold, one of his closest companions betrayed him and you say he was hailed as king. Then, in a week's time, cries of 'Crucify him! Crucify him!'? As David said, 'Those who hate me without a cause are more than the hairs of my head; Those who would destroy me are powerful, being wrongfully my enemies; what I did not steal, I then have to restore.'"[26] The man, thinking on these things, then concluded, "It seems to me the crowds, those of his own people who turned on him, were blinded to who he was."

"Blinded! Yes, blinded! That's just what they were!" Cleopas said in a tone as if something had just dawned on him. "Although Yeshua had performed so many signs before them, their rejection of him surely proved their unbelief."

Then Cleopas, as if catching himself, added, "Don't misunderstand me; many people did believe in him, including many of the Jewish leaders. But they would not admit it for fear the Pharisees would expel them from the synagogue. It was quite obvious that they loved human praise more than the praise of God, but I was thinking of those who did reject him."[27]

"Cleopas, you seem as a man who's just realized a truth," the stranger observed.

"Actually, I was thinking of Isaiah. Could this mean…," Cleopas's words came haltingly.

The man quickly nodded, as if knowing Cleopas's thoughts. "What Isaiah said concerning their blindness?" Cleopas gave a slight, slow nod of his head. The man offered a caring grin as he assured, "Indeed, 'Make the heart of this people calloused; make their ears dull and close their eyes. Otherwise they might see with their eyes, hear with their ears, understand with their hearts, and turn and be healed.'[28] I see you are now connecting these things. That's good… Very good."

I could see that Cleopas felt affirmed. Could there have been a slight bit of light shining behind our dark cloud? I suddenly felt more comfortable with the array of Scriptures that not only our traveling companion presented, but what seemed to come to my own mind and now even to my longtime friend's. For the first time, I saw Cleopas's expression relax, as though he was a bit more open and trusting instead of his usual combative self.

The Messiah Would Suffer

Still walking steadily onward, the man reviewed aloud, "Your Yeshua, as you tell me, was betrayed by a close friend, rejected by his own people, and despised by the religious leaders. All of which we know was foretold by Moses and the prophets, correct?" he queried as he counted off this unfortunate list upon his fingers.

"Quite true on all counts," I sadly confirmed.

"And what of his own family?" he asked. "Did they believe in him?"

"Well, his brothers did *not* believe in him; they were not supportive," I said.

"Indeed they were not," Cleopas interjected with a strong tone. "I remember, perhaps you will to," Cleopas said, motioning to me, "that day in Galilee when *Sukkot*, the Feast of Booths, was near?"

I nodded, "How could I forget?"

"You see," Cleopas explained to the man, "his brothers, his own brothers, said to him, 'Leave here and go into Judea, so that your disciples also may see your works, which you are doing,'" Cleopas's shoulders bounced as he repeated their words in an overly animated fashion. He continued his imitation, "'For no one does anything in secret when he himself seeks to be known publicly. If you do these things, show yourself to the world.'"[29]

"That is just what they said. His own brothers! Once, when his family heard he was healing others and that large crowds had come to follow him—to the point that even if he stopped for a meal he was unable to eat—they tried to take custody of him saying, 'He's out of his mind!'"[30]

"Now, Cleopas." Again, the stranger had this uncanny tenderness for my friend's frustration. He seemed to know just what was needed to soothe the spirit. "Do you remember what Eliab said to young David, to the one who would eventually be king?"

Cleopas looked embarrassingly puzzled. "Eliab, Eliab," he repeated to himself as if searching his memory.

"Eliab was David's oldest brother. Do you remember what happened when he heard David speaking to the other men, the other soldiers, concerning what should be done for the person who defeated Goliath? Eliab's anger burned against David as he falsely accused him."

Suddenly, the man took on the same animation as Cleopas did when he imitated Yeshua's brothers, "'Why have you come down? And with whom have you left those few sheep in the wilderness? I know your insolence and the wickedness of your heart; for you have come down in order to see the battle.'"[31]

I could see through the embarrassment a slight grin had overcome Cleopas, one he was obviously trying to mask. The man continued in his normal tone, "David's heart was pure in that he only sought to honor God. Neither David's brothers, nor Joseph's brothers, who sold him as a slave, could at first accept the possibility of the great calling God had placed upon their own brother's heart and life. No," he said shaking his head knowingly, "a prophet is not without honor except in his hometown, among his own relatives, and in his own household."[32]

Cleopas and I just looked at each other, feeling quite certain we had heard that somewhere before!

"But King David's brothers, as well as Joseph's, eventually came around. Be patient. I believe the brothers of Yeshua will also come around." Then, looking heavenward as if deep in thought, he uttered the words from a psalm of David, "May those who wait for you not be ashamed through me, O LORD God of hosts; May those who seek you not be dishonored through me, O God of Israel, because for your sake I have borne reproach; dishonor has covered my face. I have become estranged from my brothers and an alien to my mother's sons."[33]

Amazed, I felt myself staring at the man. He then said to me, as if coming out of a daydream, "Ah, let us continue our journey."

It was once again exciting to me, as he quoted the psalm, the incredible accuracy of the Scripture to the situation. My mind pondered these things for a while as we walked along. I soon found that my constant nervous excitement was only compounded by the fact that my stomach was getting the better of me as the sun began to set on our journey. Cleopas's desire for food had left him since Yeshua's arrest just days before. Mine however—well, stress tended to increase my appetite.

When I think of those times, those wonderful times with Yeshua—seeing him, hearing him speak to the people, oh, his love for the people—it fills me with joy. But when I think of the twelve and the others, it makes me chuckle, remembering how our stomachs never seemed to agree at the same time as to when we should break bread. How often one of the men in our group, at varying times and circumstances, usually asked, "Have we got anything here to eat?" Oh, how the women chided us about this. Of course, we usually had a loaf to pass around or figs, dates, or other such things to eat.

Yet, I remember, on one particular day when Yeshua had surprised us by conversing with a Samaritan woman by the well of Jacob. We all urged him to eat something. But he said to us in that easy tone of his, "I have food to eat that you do not know about." As usual we were greatly puzzled, so we began to ask one another, "No one brought him anything to eat, did he?" Then Yeshua tenderly reminded us, "My food is to do the will of him who sent me and to accomplish his work."[34] Of course it was.

I must have had a grin on my face as I recalled these things because suddenly I realized Cleopas was glaring at me. I hate to catch myself when I am not paying attention, let alone when someone else catches me. But I know Cleopas's heart is that I not lose an opportunity to learn, to understand. *My dear Cleopas, my trusted friend.*

"I guess we are no better than those who rejected him openly," Cleopas confessed angrily.

I was greatly puzzled as to why Cleopas would suddenly say this to me so sharply. "What do you mean by that?"

"And what of us?" Cleopas asked and then answered, "Yes, Judas betrayed him; Peter denied him, cursing that he ever knew Yeshua; and the rest of us? Scattered like rats in a room at the lighting of an oil lamp."

I hung my head. I knew Cleopas was right. Could this have been the real reason for the sharp look? The stranger glanced back and forth at us as we walked with him. We were now quite silent. Our hearts were as heavy as when we began our journey, yet now filled with condemnation.

The man once again placed his hands upon our shoulders as he walked between us. Then he spoke tenderly, "Do you not know the words of Zechariah? 'Awake, O sword, against my shepherd, and against the man, my associate,' declares the LORD of hosts. 'Strike the shepherd that the sheep may be scattered.'[35] And King David's words, 'My heart throbs, my strength fails me; and the light of my eyes, even that has gone from me. My loved ones and my friends stand aloof from my plague; and my kinsmen stand afar off.'"[36]

"Even that?" I asked with surprise.

"Even that," said the man with pity in his eyes for our pain.

I reflected on this for a moment and then glanced over to Cleopas for his reaction, but instead I could see in his face that rather familiar calculating look, as if he were going to pose something. He was quite good at outwitting others with his strong intellect. He loved to sit with the elders at the gate and spar academically on some religious topic of concern. Oh, the questions he would raise. He was a bit older than I was, and I guess I had hoped that some of his sharp intellect would rub off on me. Somehow, I never quite felt as though it ever did.

"If I may," Cleopas put forward to the man with an uncharacteristic hesitancy, "I must go back to what you mentioned earlier as we conversed. You said that it was 'necessary' for Messiah to suffer these things. Are these *all* the things he was to suffer? Do you mean the pain of all this rejection and hatred? That is what you mean, isn't it? Surely, you cannot mean, I mean, surely…"

"Surely, I cannot mean that the long-awaited one would be handed over to the Gentiles for crucifixion specifically? I tell you that is exactly what I mean." The man declared this stunning revelation matter-of-factly. We looked at him and gasped in utter disbelief and astonishment. To convince us of this, that Messiah's crucifixion was actually foretold, would certainly take some serious convincing.

How the Messiah Would Suffer

Although we continued to walk together, the weight of the man's last statement, that Messiah's crucifixion was actually foretold, hung heavily in the air above us. The awful pressure of the implication of this made us feel as if we were attempting to breathe through the steam of a boiling hot spring. The stranger, breaking the suffocating silence, stated gently, "I see in your faces, aside from astonishment at my last statement, a familiar pain. It is as when I first came upon you."

What could we say? Once again, the man was right. We knew that if we followed his line of reasoning, the next subject would be the one we'd never want to think on again, let alone discuss in all its horrific detail. Did we really want to delve into this? Was our desire for an answer greater than our desire to forget the horror of it all? To be honest, I just wasn't sure.

"You do not want to recount his physical suffering. I understand that," he said with compassion. "However, arriving at truth can sometimes be painful. That is why so many people avoid it. The process, the road to truth, can be painful. But truth must be pursued, no matter how painful at first.

"There is freedom in knowing truth. Thus, we need to talk about *how* he suffered, in spite of the enormous difficulty in recounting it, so that you can see that it was indeed in God's plan. We will then talk about *why* he suffered, so you can understand the purpose."

"*The truth will set you free,*" I recalled Yeshua's words, and they confirmed the man's suggestion. We've come this far in seeing the Scriptures speak on so much concerning the one we loved, trusted, and believed. I knew—we knew—though painful to recall, we ought to continue. "Yes," I said softly. "Yes, we must go on." Cleopas nodded slowly and solemnly.

Our traveling companion nodded as well, while he tenderly said, "Then, let us continue our discussion. Now, the prophet Isaiah said, 'His appearance was marred more than any man and his form more than the sons of men.'[37] Tell me what you know, what you witnessed. How was Yeshua marred more than any man and his form, or body, more than the sons of men?"

At this point, he wasn't holding back on specifically applying the Scriptures to our Yeshua. There was now no argument from us on this approach. There were too many Scriptures that perfectly applied; all of them really. Again, it would have been folly to argue with him otherwise.

Cleopas glanced over to me, obviously wanting me to begin with my own recollection. I shook my head after a moment and gestured that he should begin. I couldn't. Not just yet. Cleopas cleared his throat, took a deep breath, and then explained, "Of course, the Roman soldiers were not going to be gentle with him after his arrest in the garden. But at the trial before Caiaphas, when he declared Yeshua had committed blasphemy and all declared him worthy of death, they spat in his face and struck him with their fists. Others blindfolded him and slapped his face as they yelled mockingly, 'Now you, Messiah, prophesy to us: who hit you that time?'"[38] For the first time Cleopas's voice cracked. He looked straight ahead to the sinking sun.

I could not help but to think back to the binding of Yeshua by his captors. During the very time he was bound and tried, the standing barley was also bound in preparation for it to be reaped the following evening. Once reaped the barley was brought to the priests in the Temple three baskets full, a full sheaf's worth, or omer— enough to fulfill the mandate of our Law. So on went those who prepare for this feast as if nothing else were happening in Jerusalem; on went the preparation for the First Fruits offering.

I looked toward Cleopas and seeing he was unable to continue, I swallowed hard and then shared, "Pilate had him scourged with thirty-nine lashes. The amount that is believed to be one less than what would kill a man." There was no need to go into detail regarding the cruelty of the Roman scourging. The whip, having metal balls that severely bruised Yeshua's skin and sharp bones that then tore into his flesh from the top of his shoulders to the back of his legs, left him with a tremendous loss of blood, and his skin literally flayed.[39]

I continued, "After the scourging, with his body a quivering mass of blood and torn flesh, the soldiers then mocked him. They pressed hard upon his precious head a twisted crown made up of long sharp thorns. The soldiers then stripped him of his own garments and replaced them with a scarlet robe. Then with a reed they had placed in his hand as a mock scepter, they beat Yeshua about the head."

The man then offered softly, "As Isaiah said, 'I gave my back to those who strike me, and my cheeks to those who pluck out the beard; I did not cover my face from humiliation and spitting. For the LORD God helps me, therefore, I am not disgraced; therefore, I have set my face like flint, and I know that I will not be ashamed.'"[40]

As odd as it may sound, his quotation of Isaiah actually comforted me. Yeshua's face *had been* set like a flint. As much as one could maintain a dignity through such torture, I have to say he did. But at this point of our conversation, I also had a renewed confidence and awe in the Holy Scriptures and in the true and living God who inspired them.

"What happened after he was mocked in the scarlet robe?" he asked.

I glanced over to Cleopas, almost asking permission to be the one to speak on the matter. He nodded in my direction, gesturing for me to continue. I felt I could go on now because I knew we were not conversing about these things for the sake of talking about them. There was a purpose to our discussion, which gave me the strength to continue. It felt good to have Cleopas defer to me.

"They then replaced the scarlet robe with his own garments and led him out for crucifixion. Now, of course due to his loss of blood, Yeshua staggered badly, as he was forced to carry the cross-beam. He then collapsed, and one, Simon of Cyrene, helped him to carry it the rest of the way to Golgotha.

"There Yeshua then offered—yes, he actually offered the Roman soldiers—his hands and feet as they pierced his flesh, hammering the large spikes into them." My voice trailed off, "No struggle to fight against the soldiers, no attempt to escape their grasp as there was with the two other men who were with him in crucifixion although we could certainly hear his agony as they pounded those spikes through the flesh and nerves of his hands and feet."

As I somberly pondered these things, my mind wandered to something Yeshua had said while with us. I could almost hear his voice as I recalled it in my mind. "For this reason the Father loves me, because I lay down my life so that I may take it up again. No one has taken it away from me, but I lay it down on my own initiative. I have authority to lay it down, and I have authority to take it up again. This commandment I received from my Father."[41]

And I recalled the women proclaiming his tomb empty. But I was getting ahead of myself; first things first. It must be proven to me that the Scriptures could actually speak of such a horribly tortuous death for one so innocent.

My mind once again returned to the priest's preparation for First Fruits. They relentlessly threshed, roasted, and sifted the barley through thirteen sieves to create the fine flour used to make the bread offering. So, too, our Yeshua was beaten and bruised, sifted by his interrogators before being led out to crucifixion.

"Yes," I admitted to our informed companion. "Your quote from Isaiah was accurate. Yeshua's appearance *was* marred more than any man and his body more than the sons of men."

"Indeed, indeed," he said as he gently nodded in affirmation. "And let us continue. Now, tell me the events of what happened once crucified."

I looked at the man as he attempted to move the conversation along in such a tender way. I cannot explain this, but I felt that even though I did not know him, I could trust him with my deepest pain, and this was certainly it.

I continued as instructed, "The soldiers, after they had crucified him, gave him wine to drink mixed with gall or myrrh. After tasting it, he was unwilling to drink it. It was a type of poison, you see, that they use to help alleviate the suffering of those they crucify." I thought for a moment on this and then added quizzically, "That seems quite contradictory, doesn't it? To torture a man literally from head to toe and then offer him something for pain?"

"Quite contrary," he said as he nodded in agreement. The man then queried, "And of those who hated him? What of their presence? Surely they were there?"

"Oh yes, they made themselves quite known," Cleopas broke in, once again engaged. His disgust over the behavior of the religious leaders could not easily be hidden. "The chief priests and scribes acted no better than the Roman soldiers who, at the foot of his cross as he was suspended in agony, divided up his only possessions—his garments. They made sport by casting lots among themselves to see who would be the winner of them."

I sighed and said with equal disgust, "Oh, yes. When they had crucified Yeshua, the soldiers took his outer garments and made four parts, a part to each soldier. Then they took his tunic. But because it was seamless, woven in one piece, they said to one another, 'Let's not tear it, but cast lots for it, to decide whose it shall be.'[42]

"Those passing by were hurling abusive words at him, shaking their heads and saying, 'You who are going to destroy the Temple and rebuild it in three days, save yourself! If you are the Son of God, come down from the cross.'"[43]

Cleopas quickly interjected, "And what about the chief priests and scribes and elders?" He turned to our traveling companion and said passionately, "In the same way they all were mocking him and saying, 'He saved others; he cannot save himself. He is the King of Israel; let him now come down from the cross, and we will believe in him. He trusts in God; let God rescue him now, if he delights in him; for he said, "I am the Son of God."'

"Many others just stood there staring at him as if entertaining themselves by him in all his humiliation."

I then added, "There was no escape from the continual scoffing. Even the criminals, one on the right side of him and one on the left, were insulting him with the same words. But then a bit later, one of them turned to Yeshua in belief. Cleopas, do you remember?"

"Yes," Cleopas said. "Yes, I do. I will never forget. He said to the man who then put his trust in Yeshua, 'Truly I say to you, today you shall be with me in Paradise.'"[44]

"And to those who crucified him? His words to them were…?" the man asked almost knowingly. It felt as if he wanted us to speak these words aloud.

Cleopas and I looked at each other past the man who was still between us. We then said in unison and rather solemnly, "Father, forgive them; for they do not know what they are doing."[45]

We then fell silent. It was obvious the stranger wanted us to ponder Yeshua's words for a long while. I thought to myself, *Could I utter such words under such circumstances?* No ordinary man could. Then again, it was obvious that Yeshua was no ordinary man.

Breaking the unbearable silence, "Eventually he did die," the man said, prompting us to continue.

I looked at him and nodded in affirmation then explained, "From noon until three o'clock in the afternoon, all the land was covered with darkness. At about three, Yeshua uttered a loud cry, *'Eli! Eli! L'mah sh'vaktani?'* That is 'My God! My God! Why have you deserted me?'

"This confused the people, as they thought he was calling for Elijah. Then he said, 'I am thirsty.' A jar full of sour wine, or vinegar, was standing there, so they soaked a sponge in it, placed the sponge upon a branch of hyssop, and brought it up to his mouth. When Yeshua had received it, he spoke his last words, 'It is finished! Father, into your hands I commit my spirit.' And with that, he bowed his head and gave up his spirit."

I continued with difficulty, it seemed that boulder in my throat had returned. "Then the Jews, because it was the day of preparation and so that the bodies would not remain on the cross on the Sabbath, asked Pilate to have their legs broken so they could be taken away. The soldiers came and broke the legs of the first man and of the other who was crucified with him to hasten their deaths. You see, they could not then lift up on the spike that was through their feet, which would have allowed them to exhale. In no time they asphyxiated. But coming to Yeshua, when they saw that he was already dead, they did not break his legs."

I looked to the man as I assured, "The soldiers know death. They caused enough and have seen enough to know he was dead. But instead of breaking the legs of a man who was already dead, I think really just to confirm to the crowd, one of the soldiers pierced his side with a spear, and immediately blood and water came out, certainly the sign of death."[46]

Cleopas, realizing the increased difficulty I had when sharing these things, interjected, "When it was evening, a rich man, Joseph from Arimathea, a follower of Yeshua and a member of the Sanhedrin, went to Pilate and asked for Yeshua's body, and Pilate, thankfully, ordered it to be given to him. Joseph then took Yeshua's body, wrapped it in a clean linen cloth, and laid it in his own new tomb, which he had hewn out in the rock. He rolled a large stone against the entrance of the tomb and went away."[47]

We walked along for a while attempting to maintain some sort of composure before the man. It wasn't easy. I felt exhausted and empty as if I had run a long race but just missed the coveted wreath. Then he finally spoke, "My friends, the first thing you recalled of his words upon the cruel cross were, 'My God! My God! Why have you deserted me?'"

Cleopas said, with a slight edge in his voice that seemed to return from the beginning of our journey, "Yes, yes. He was in agony. Why wouldn't he call to ADONAI? Look at what had transpired. Why shouldn't he feel deserted?"

"But my friends," the stranger posed gingerly, "Does that not sound familiar to you both? Do you not remember learning the psalm as children?"

We thought for a moment. Then suddenly Cleopas and I stopped dead in our tracks. We looked at each other and said in unison, "My God! My God! Why have you deserted me?" We stood there with our mouths agape as we grabbed each other by the forearms. Indeed we had heard and learned that psalm as children. Cleopas and I struggled to remember it word for word as we offered passages from it back and forth.

"For I am a worm and not a man..."

"... I am despised by the people, they sneer..."

"... I am poured out like water..."

"... my bones,... uh... my bones are..."

Cleopas and I clumsily tried to finish the verse the other had started. My heart pounded with excitement. The man stood there with a smile on his face from his position slightly ahead of us on the road.

After clearing his throat loudly, to gain our attention, he said, "Then, you do remember it." He knew that, for a moment, we had forgotten not only the important parts of the psalm, but also that our traveling companion was even there as we were caught up in our spontaneous exchange. "My dear friends, let's take the pertinent parts of the psalm and apply them as they should be, shall we?" he said politely but with some emphasis in an attempt to gain our attention.

"Yes, yes, of course. Forgive us our excitement," Cleopas said as he tried to compose his usually dignified self. I felt the need to adjust my tunic and the mantle upon my shoulders because we had had each other in a tight grasp around our sleeves. Cleopas did the same. I was sure my arms had bruises on them because Cleopas was not only intellectually, but also physically stronger as well.

"Your excitement is a blessing," the man said, maintaining his casual smile. "But we do need to break down the psalm so you can see clearly."

"Yes," Cleopas said, "forgive us. Please tell us as we seem to need *clarity*."

"Indeed," the stranger nodded. "Yeshua was quoting a psalm of David. These passages clearly speak of his crucifixion, of that there can be no doubt, by your own account of the events. David wrote, 'My God, my God, why have you forsaken me? Far from my deliverance are the words of my groaning. But I am a worm and not a man, a reproach of men and despised by the people. All who see me sneer at me; they separate with the lip, they wag the head, saying, "Commit yourself to the LORD; let him deliver him; let him rescue him, because he delights in him."' David went on to write, 'I am poured out like water, and all my bones are out of joint.'"

"Yes, his bones were out of joint—that's one of the things crucifixion does. Cleopas, the bones go out of joint from the weight of the suspended body when the arms are outstretched," I shared with passion.

The man continued speaking passages from the psalm, "'My heart is like wax; it is melted within me...'"

"Cleopas," I said, "the blood and water from his heart was exposed by the spear to his side."

Cleopas nodded in my direction quickly as the man continued, "'My strength is dried up like a potsherd, and my tongue cleaves to my jaws; and you lay me in the dust of death. For dogs have surrounded me; a band of evildoers has encompassed me; they pierced my hands and my feet...'"

"Of course, they did! That's just what they did!" I couldn't contain myself.

Unaffected by my zeal, the stranger went on, "'I can count all my bones...'"

"Yes, he could; none of his bones were broken." I excitedly told the man. Then, turning to my dear friend, "Remember, Cleopas, they did not break his legs as they did with the others!"

"Yes, I remember, now let him continue," Cleopas said as he lightly rebuked me, gesturing toward the man.

The stranger continued with the psalm, "'They look, they stare at me; they divide my garments among them, and for my clothing they cast lots.'"[48]

I couldn't help myself, "The Roman soldiers… the soldiers!"

"Yes, yes, I know," Cleopas said in his attempt to hush me, tapping his hand in the air as you would the top of a child's head.

The man nodded in my direction then added, "Another psalm of David speaks thus, 'Reproach has broken my heart and I am so sick. And I looked for sympathy, but there was none, and for comforters, but I found none. They also gave me gall for my food and for my thirst they gave me vinegar to drink.'"[49]

"Amazing, absolutely amazing!" Cleopas said with vigor as he shook his head. He was now unable to contain himself.

The man agreed, "Yes, the Scriptures are accurate, foretelling hundreds of years before the events, including what you mentioned regarding one Joseph of Arimathea. Isaiah wrote, 'His grave was assigned with wicked men, yet he was with a rich man in his death, because he had done no violence, nor was there any deceit in his mouth.'[50] And by the way, crucifixion, as a method of execution, actually does strike the heel; which, of course, brings us back to the serpent in the garden, which we discussed earlier in our journey."

"It's incredible, Cleopas, that all of this was foretold. How could we have missed it?" I could not express my excitement enough. Then suddenly, I saw the expression on Cleopas's face change. "Cleopas," I said, trying to get his attention. I knew that distant gaze. "Don't you think this is incredible?"

Cleopas took a deep breath and looked at me. It was almost as if he hated to say what he needed to say. I could see it in his face. "What is it, Cleopas? What's wrong?" My shoulders sank.

"We have more to discuss," our informed traveling companion stated matter-of-factly as he looked straight down the dusty road that would eventually take us to Emmaus.

Cleopas explained, "It is not as though I do not see in the Scriptures what our Yeshua endured, but we *do* have more to discuss, don't we?" The man gently nodded as Cleopas continued, "I am now no longer worried about the pain of recounting these things if you tell me there is a *reason* for his physical suffering." Cleopas seemed resigned, "I am ready to accept what you say fully if you can show me where all this makes sense. I just want to know that it was not in vain. That our Yeshua's physical suffering was not in vain."

Suddenly, I felt as if I were jerked back into reality. But Cleopas was right. We've only talked about *how* he suffered. The real issue at hand was *why*.

Why the Messiah Would Suffer

I could feel a slight breeze in the air as the long afternoon was ending. I put my head back and breathed deeply the refreshing air that carried the scents from the Judean Mountains. Although our pace was not rushed, the light air was pleasing as we traveled to our hometown. We needed a bit of refreshment as we began the task of delving into the subject of *why* Yeshua suffered so. Nothing seemed to matter more in our discussion thus far, because we knew that if we had clarity on this, it would indeed change our thinking, and yes, even our lives.

"Cleopas, do you remember when I first happened upon you," the man asked. "I said that Moses and the prophets spoke of his suffering?"

"Yes," Cleopas said, "and we've discussed that. But now we must know *why*." His emphasis on the word *why* revealed a mild frustration, kind of an underlying *Get to the point, please!* attitude.

"Do you remember that I also said Moses and the prophets not only spoke of his suffering, but also of his being the *final atoning sacrifice necessary for the sin of the world?*" The stranger spoke these words slowly and deliberately. We had to think back. We were so focused on the fact that he had referred to Yeshua as Messiah and then to the role of King that I don't think this comment even registered in our minds; *The final atoning sacrifice necessary for the sin of the world.* He continued, "You want to know the *why* of his suffering. I will tell you plainly as he told you plainly. But first, Cleopas, you must see that atonement has always been by blood sacrifice. Without the shedding of blood, there is no forgiveness.[51]

"Moses, noting the words of ADONAI, proclaimed, 'For the life of a creature is in the blood, and I have given it to you on the altar to make atonement for yourselves; for it is the blood that makes atonement because of the life.'[52]

"Blood atonement, throughout the Scriptures, cannot be missed. As you know, Temple sacrifices are for the individual, Passover for the family, and the Day of

Atonement for the sin of the nation. The purpose of the Messiah was to render the final perfect atonement for the sin of the world.

"And, Cleopas, the idea of substitutionary atonement is indeed throughout the *Tanakh* as well. Blood was shed to cover Adam and Eve's sin and shame. Abel's blood sacrifice, a substitute, was accepted as atonement for his sin. Abraham offered Isaac as a sacrifice for his sin; the ram died as a substitute. The lamb's blood on the doorpost was a substitutionary sacrifice for the firstborn of Israel. Annually, on Yom Kippur, two sacrificial goats provide atonement between Israel and God. And the Messiah shed his blood, the perfect Lamb of God, not to cover sin as the Temple sacrifices did, but to take it away forever and reconcile the relationship with God that was broken in the Garden."

My mind raced back to John the Immerser's comments one day in the Jordan, regarding Yeshua. "Behold the Lamb of God who takes away the sin of the world,"[53] *the Lamb of God*, of course!

"Cleopas," the stranger asked, "why do you think John the Immerser referred to Yeshua as the *Lamb of God who takes away the sin of the world?*" Cleopas's eyes were wide. For the first time since I've known him—all my life that is—this man who stumps most with his intellect was quite speechless. I could see this was something that just had not occurred to him. Not that it had occurred to me immediately either, but there are many things that do not occur to me. However, I have grown rather accustomed to that.

"And why, Cleopas, do you think John the Immerser said this?" the man pressed. "Why do you think he called Yeshua 'the Lamb of God'? What is the Lamb's role?"

Once again I recalled the trial, Yeshua's demeanor as he stood before our leaders and then to the Scripture that had come to my mind before. *"He was oppressed and he was afflicted, yet he did not open his mouth; like a lamb that is led to slaughter, and like a sheep that is silent before its shearers, so he did not open his mouth."*[54]

Then it hit me. I realized it for the first time. It hit me like a great wave crashing upon the shore. "Isaiah, Isaiah," I heard myself say aloud, my breathing became heavy, "Cleopas," I said with a whisper, now *my* voice cracked. I had a hard time catching my breath.

"Yes, yes," Cleopas answered with a concerned yet puzzled tone. "What is it? What is wrong with you? Are you ill, my friend?"

"Isaiah… ," was all I could say. The man, who always seemed to position himself between us, grabbed hold of my arm. The moment he touched me I knew, as my eyes pooled with tears, that I could never get the words out with any clarity to my dear friend, Cleopas. Yet, as I felt the firm grip upon my arm, I also knew—I tell you I knew—he could explain what was in my heavily pounding heart so much better than I ever could.

And as if prompted, the man spoke, "'Behold, my servant will prosper, he will be high and lifted up and greatly exalted. Just as many were astonished at you, my people, so his appearance was marred more than any man and his form more than the sons of men. Thus he will sprinkle many nations. Kings will shut their mouths on account of him; for what had not been told them they will see, and what they had not heard they will understand.'" He was almost poetic in his tone, yet his voice spoke with great determination.

The man continued reciting Isaiah flawlessly from memory, "'He was despised and forsaken of men, a man of sorrows and acquainted with grief; and like one from whom men hide their face. He was despised, and we did not esteem him.'"

Cleopas's eyes were wide; his breathing pattern began to match mine, as I could see upon his face the realization and significance of what the stranger spoke so eloquently.

We slowly stopped walking and found ourselves facing him in the middle of the road, once again with our mouths agape.

"'Surely our grief he himself bore, and our sorrows he carried; yet we ourselves esteemed him stricken, smitten of God, and afflicted.'"

The man stepped closer to us then said methodically, "'But he was pierced through for our transgressions. He was crushed for our iniquities; the chastening for our well-being fell upon him, and by his scourging we are healed. All of us like sheep have gone astray, each of us has turned to his own way; but the LORD has caused the iniquity of us all to fall on him.'"

He then slowly turned his head and looked directly at me as he recited, "'He was oppressed and he was afflicted, yet he did not open his mouth; like a lamb that is led to slaughter, and like a sheep that is silent before its shearers, so he did not open his mouth.'"

I covered my face with my hands as I felt the tears pour into my palms. My shoulders jolted up and down as I wept silently into my hands. I could feel Cleopas's hand upon my back. He stood there silent as the man continued, "By oppression and judgment he was taken away; and as for his generation, who considered that he was cut off out of the land of the living for the transgression of my people, to whom the stroke was due?'"

The stranger then gently took hold of my wrists and moved my hands down and away from my face. He paused for me to compose myself somewhat, and then looking directly at us, he continued quoting Isaiah, "'But the LORD was pleased to crush him, putting him to grief; if he would render himself as a guilt offering, he will see his offspring, he will prolong his days, and the good pleasure of the LORD will prosper in his hand. As a result of the anguish of his soul, he will see it and be satisfied; by his knowledge the righteous one, my servant, will justify the many, as he will bear their iniquities.'"

Then, stepping once more between us, hands once again on our shoulders, he walked us down the road as he concluded, "'Therefore, I will allot him a portion with the great, and he will divide the booty with the strong; because he poured out himself to death, and was numbered with the transgressors; yet he himself bore the sin of many, and interceded for the transgressors.'"[55]

"Oh, Cleopas," I managed to finally get something out, "'*he interceded for the transgressors.*' What comes to your mind, Cleopas? What does that bring you back to?"

Cleopas said, "Yes, I know. 'Forgive them Father; for they do not know what they are doing.' And so he came, yes, Messiah. Not only as the High Priest to offer the sacrifice, but to *be* the sacrificial Lamb of God as well. True?"

"It is as you've said," the man assured.

We walked a bit farther in silence as our minds adjusted to the revelation that not only confirmed that Yeshua was the Messiah, but specifically prophesied as the Suffering Servant of whom Isaiah the prophet spoke. Cleopas then confessed, "I had always thought those words of Isaiah—well that we, that Israel, was the Suffering Servant of Isaiah. It just seemed to me that we, as a people, suffer at the hands of those who brutally persecute us simply for being who we are. I never imagined that the King we waited for, who would save Israel, would suffer so."

"No, Cleopas, the Scripture states plainly that the person spoken of by Isaiah is a singular male figure," the man explained, "not a group. Besides, Isaiah the prophet was speaking of his own people when he used the words *we* and *us*. It is at those times that he was speaking of Israel specifically. No, the servant in Isaiah came to save you from your sin and from yourselves. Do you see that?"

"Yes, I see that now. I do see that now." Cleopas

answered in the most reserved and humbled tone that I had ever heard from him.

"You were quite right, Cleopas, when you said he came to be the High Priest to offer the sacrifice and to fulfill the sacrifice by shedding his own blood. The priests sacrifice year after year, but Isaiah spoke of him who would be one sacrifice for the sin of many—one final atoning sacrifice," the man confirmed.

He then went on to say, "You mentioned earlier that at the ninth hour, at three o'clock, he cried out with a loud voice and uttered, 'It is finished,' and breathed his last. My friends, that is exactly when the sacrifice was being made for the Passover. And when he came into Jerusalem on a donkey's colt, it was of course the same day of the selection for the sacrifice. Could he have communicated why he came any clearer?"

"He did make it clear, very clear. Oh, Cleopas, when I think about his words now, so much of what he said points to these conclusions. Why could we not see it?" I said with my own frustration, not at our traveling companion for revealing these obvious things or even at Cleopas, but at myself.

Cleopas then uttered to himself, "Not a bone of him was broken. They did not break his bones."

"What?" I asked wondering where Cleopas was going with this thought that seemed quite out of the blue. It seemed he didn't even hear what I had said and the manner in which I said it.

"The Passover Lamb, no bone of it, according to the Law of Moses, was to be broken. I just recalled a line in a psalm of David, 'He keeps all his bones, not one of them is broken.'[56] Even that was fulfilled, they did not break his bones." Cleopas let out a heavy sigh then said, "Why could we not see it? How could we have missed so much when he made it so clear?"

"That's what I said." I interjected feeling as if I were being ignored. But I do understand Cleopas's distraction.

The man then reminded, "Has not ADONAI always provided for his people? After all, he provided a pillar of cloud by day, a pillar of fire by night, water from the rock, manna from heaven, dry land across the Red Sea, and the perfect final sacrifice for the sin of the world. Indeed, 'It is finished.' Has not he always provided?"

Cleopas nodded with a pleased resignation and then answered, "I believe he has."

The man then asked, "So why should he suddenly stop now?"

"Hum. Good point, huh, Cleopas?" I chided.

The Messiah's Resurrection

Nearing the end of our journey, we could see the tops of the trees reflecting the sun, which had slipped below the horizon. As we walked, Cleopas was shaking his head. "It seems we witnessed so much yet understood so little," he finally concluded.

I nodded with an embarrassed agreement. I could see the chariot wheels turning in Cleopas's head. He always needed to have things in an order that made sense. This was why I think he was so good at argumentation. He always seemed to grasp what was missing in a particular line of reasoning. His sharp mind amazed me. I guess that was why it amused me a bit to see him grapple with what was right in front of him physically yet far from his usually keen mind.

As I mentioned before, I was accustomed to missing the obvious.

Cleopas vigorously rubbed his face with his hands as if washing the dust off of it in an attempt to clear his mind. Then, trying to pull everything together, he posed, "So Yeshua was born as a human, 'a child would be born unto us,' yet he was fully God. His miracles, wisdom, and power proclaimed thus, that he is indeed 'Preeminent over eternity.'"

"Yes, I have to agree," I said speaking past the man. Then I added, "Remember when he told the Pharisees, 'Before Abraham was born *I AM*'?"[57] I then leaned into the stranger, "They wanted to stone him for that right then and there. Because not only was he saying that he existed before Abraham did, but also that he was the *I AM*, well… that he was God! But he somehow escaped them and went his way." The man grinned a casual sort of knowing grin as he slowly nodded.

"Please, my friend," Cleopas said to me with mild irritation but as gingerly as possible, "I am trying to fully understand."

"Sorry." I didn't want to interrupt his thought process even though finishing his thoughts usually helped me to clarify mine.

Cleopas went on to ask the man, "You quoted Isaiah's words, 'He was despised, and we did not esteem him.' I must admit, our people did *not* esteem him, especially because he was handed over to the Gentiles for crucifixion. However, I know now that this was planned to redeem us from our sin. For indeed Isaiah's words are true, 'All of us like sheep *have* gone astray, each of us *has* turned to his own way.'

"There is no doubt that *all* of us sin; we constantly go opposite of where God would have us go, following our own will instead of God's. Yes, there is none righteous before God. So to remedy this, 'The LORD has caused the iniquity of us all to fall on him.' But I need to know, I must know. Is Yeshua's sacrifice for us alone or is it, dare I ask this, also for the Gentiles?"

I then said, tapping my finger in the air as my mind raced a thousand miles a second, "Umm, Cleopas, Cleopas, I think I know the answer."

"I was asking *our traveling companion* to explain," Cleopas said in his fatherly voice.

"But Cleopas, I am curious to hear what your friend has to say," the man interrupted as he moved his arm slightly across the front of Cleopas. He then gestured for me to share my thoughts on the answer to Cleopas's question.

I cleared my throat, "Uh, yes...let me see," I was suddenly nervous again, surprised that I would be allowed to answer such a heady question. But I felt as if I did know, from Yeshua's own words, what the answer was.

I went on to answer to the man, "I remember Nicodemus, one who did not want to outwardly proclaim Yeshua but met with him during the night. He was a Pharisee, you see, and I imagine he did not want the other religious leaders seeing him with Yeshua or with those who followed him. But he did seem to be grappling with Yeshua's purpose and identity.

"Yeshua lovingly told Nicodemus, 'As Moses lifted up the serpent in the wilderness,' you know," I said as I gestured toward the man, "He was speaking of when God sent fiery serpents among the people and once bitten, many individuals of Israel died. So the people came to Moses and said, 'We have sinned, because we have spoken against the LORD and you. Intercede with the LORD, that he may remove the serpents from us.'

"And Moses interceded for the people. Then God said to Moses, 'Make a fiery serpent, and set it on a standard, and it shall come about that everyone who is bitten, when he looks at it, he will live.' So Moses made a bronze serpent, set it on the standard and if a serpent bit someone, when he looked to the bronze serpent," I snapped my fingers, "he lived."[58]

Cleopas then said impatiently, "I'm sure our traveling companion knows the reference. Please continue your thoughts."

"Oh, yes, I am so sorry. I guess you would know all this." Once again, I was rebuked for saying more than needed to be.

"It's all right. I appreciate what you're sharing," the man affirmed.

I smiled and said in Cleopas's direction a deliberate, "*Anyway*," and then continued, "Yeshua said, 'As Moses lifted up the serpent in the wilderness even so must the Son of Man must be lifted up, so that whoever believes in him will have eternal life. For God so loved the world that he gave his only begotten Son that whoever believes in him shall not perish but have eternal life. For God did not send the Son into the world to judge the world, but that the world might be saved through him. He who believes in him is not judged; he who does not believe has been judged already, because he has not believed in the name of the only begotten Son of God.'[59]

"Now, Yeshua was lifted up for certain, also becoming that symbol of healing for those who look to him. But he did not say that only a few who look to him or that only Israel might be saved, but God so loved the *world*. That, to me, means that whoever, Jew or Gentile, believes in him will be saved! Is that right?"

"Yes, my friend," the stranger stated boldly and then went on to share, "I told you there was a purpose for his suffering and now you know also that through his suffering there is an opportunity for the Gentiles to be saved as well. The Scriptures speak thus, 'I am the LORD, I have called you in righteousness, I will also hold you by the hand and watch over you, and I will appoint you as a covenant to the people, *as a light to the nations*, to open blind eyes, to bring out prisoners from the dungeon and those who dwell in darkness from the prison.'[60]

"ADONAI speaking through Isaiah again said, 'It is too small a thing that you should be my servant to raise up the tribes of Jacob and to restore the preserved ones of Israel; *I will also make you a light of the nations so that my salvation may reach to the end of the earth.*'"[61]

As he shared the Scriptures with us, the man emphasized the words he spoke concerning the nations.

"Right there in the *Tanakh* all this time!" Cleopas let out in exasperation.

The man continued, "To quote the psalmist, 'The stone which the builders rejected has become the chief cornerstone. This is the LORD'S doing; it is marvelous in our eyes. This is the day which the LORD has made; let us rejoice and be glad in it.'[62] Do you see that? It is the LORD'S doing—and that this is a time not for mourning but to rejoice?"

"Yes, it is the LORD'S doing, and all the world would be blessed, a light to the Gentiles." As Cleopas was stringing these thoughts together, I recalled those to whom Yeshua had ministered, those who were not of our people, to those individuals he touched.

He healed the daughter of a Canaanite woman.[63] He revealed who he was to a Samaritan woman, a person with whom we of Israel have no dealings. And I will never forget the Roman centurion in Capernaum who implored Yeshua to heal his servant, which Yeshua did, remarking to us all regarding the man's faith, "Truly I say to you, I have not found such great faith with anyone in Israel. I say to you that many will come from east and west, and recline at the table with Abraham, Isaac, and Jacob in the kingdom of heaven."[64] *Many will come from east and west.* How could we have been so blind?

"But," Cleopas said gently, "He was forsaken by many of his own? What of that?"

Our traveling companion, unmoved, said, "They may have forsaken him now, but they will turn to him as Zechariah the prophet said, 'I will pour out on the house of David and on the inhabitants of Jerusalem, the Spirit of grace and of supplication, so that they will look on me whom they have pierced; and they will mourn for him, as one mourns for an only son, and they will weep bitterly over him like the bitter weeping over a firstborn.'"[65]

Then I reminded Cleopas excitedly, "He will come again. Do you remember, Cleopas, what he told the twelve? He said, 'In my Father's house are many dwelling places; if it were not so, I would have told you; for I go to prepare a place for you. If I go and prepare a place for you, I will come again and receive you to myself, that where I am, there you may be also.'[66]

"Yeshua will return according to the Scriptures! He is King of Kings who did have several missions. While in this world he taught us how to be reconciled with God, then he died for our sin to accomplish that, and now he lives to intercede for the transgressors as Isaiah said, to be an advocate before the Father on our behalf and finally to come again as King of Kings!"

"But I have just one more question," Cleopas firmly stated. I dropped my shoulders once again. It seemed that every time I was at that level of excitement that could replace the pain of my mourning, Cleopas just had to think again. Everything seemed to be discussed that could be discussed. The thought that went through my mind was, *What could possibly be missing from the equation now?*

The man, still unmoved, asked, "And what could that be, my friend?"

Then Cleopas burst forth with, "*Where is he?*"

I then realized, *Indeed, what's missing from this equation is his body!*

"And what did your Yeshua say?" the stranger posed.

"Apparently, a lot!" Cleopas answered in clear frustration at himself. "Oh, forgive me. Go on, please."

"He said, 'For this reason the Father loves me, because I lay down my life so that I may take it again. No one has taken it away from me, but I lay it down on my own initiative. I have authority to lay it down, and I have authority to take it up again. This commandment I received from my Father.'"[67]

My head jolted in the man's direction in that these words of Yeshua had come to my mind before.

He then went on to reiterate Cleopas's question to him. "Where is he? Think, men, think," he graciously prodded. "Remember, in a psalm of David, it says, 'I have set the LORD continually before me; because he is at my right hand, I will not be shaken. Therefore my heart is glad and my glory rejoices; my flesh also will dwell securely. For you will not abandon my soul to Sheol; nor will you allow your Holy One to undergo decay.'"[68]

The man then said methodically, *"He would not allow his Holy One to undergo decay. What does that mean? Did you not say that his tomb was empty? Is that not consistent if God raised him from the dead? Is it not consistent with the one whose words you believed and trusted? What did it mean when Yeshua said, 'Destroy this temple, and in three days I will raise it up?'"*[69]

At that, I swiftly ran over to Cleopas and once again grabbed him by the forearms saying, "Cleopas, he said, do you remember what he said? 'For just as Jonah was three days and three nights in the belly of the sea monster, so will the Son of Man be three days and three nights in the heart of the earth.'"[70]

"Ah, my friend," Cleopas returned with equal excitement, "do you remember what he told the twelve regarding himself? On his way to Jericho, he took them aside and said to them, 'Behold, we are going up to Jerusalem, and all things which are written through the prophets about the Son of Man will be accomplished, for he will be handed over to the Gentiles, and will be mocked and mistreated and spit upon, and after they have scourged him, they will kill him; and the third day he will rise again!'"[71]

Cleopas's voice rose with childlike excitement.

"Yes," I confirmed, "and I also remember that at the time the twelve thought he was speaking in riddles. They did not understand what he meant, and well, neither did we. But, Cleopas, do you now know what all this means?"

"It means that Yeshua has risen from the grave!" Cleopas said excitedly, once again his eyes were like saucers.

My mind returned to this morning, to what was happening in the Temple, to the omer, the first fruits. I then put to the stranger, "So just as the barley was brought to the Temple as first fruits of the harvest," I asked hesitantly, not sure I was making the right correlation, "so too Yeshua's resurrection makes him the first fruits of the dead?"[72]

The stranger smiled and nodded, "Indeed."

"Yes, my friend, because he has risen to eternal life, we will also rise to eternal life in him!" Cleopas said confidently maintaining his excitement while locking tightly onto my forearms. We just looked at each other with huge smiles as our mouths were wide open searching for something else to say.

The man, whose presence we had once again almost forgotten because of our excitement, stared at us from his position slightly ahead, as he said, "You did mention that the women confirmed his body was gone from the tomb?"

He then cocked his head to one side as he casually asked, "Why then did you not believe them?"

We just looked at him speechless; we were rendered utterly speechless.

The Messiah
Opened Our Eyes

After a moment, we looked around and realized that we had arrived at our destination, our humble village of Emmaus. A hilly region spotted with olive trees and, of course, rocky roads layered in white dust that covered our feet and legs by the end of our rather unusual and yet enlightening journey. Suddenly, we realized the presence of people walking to and fro about us as Cleopas and I stood there with our forearms still in each other's grasp. At that moment we thought it best to let go.

"Well, it seems you have arrived at your desired destination. It was good to talk with you and walk with you by the way," our traveling companion said.

Cleopas and I once again locked eyes, our expressions screaming, *Oh no!* We realized that this was the end of our time with this man who took us on an amazing journey. We simply did not want our time with him to end… not just yet! And we certainly could not let him go without blessing him for all that he taught us.

"But," Cleopas said, "haven't you arrived at *your* destination as well?"

"No, I will continue on," the man replied as he began to turn his body to head further along the road.

"Well, well, but…" I stammered like a child. The man stopped and raised his eyebrows with a curiously quizzical expression. Cleopas looked at me as if to say, *We cannot let him go!* I felt panicked. Dumbstruck.

Cleopas stepped closer to our new friend. I was, once again, so grateful for his boldness. He then urged, pointing to his home just a few feet from where we stood, "You must allow us to bless you. Please stay with us."

"Yes, yes," I urged in like manner, "stay with us, for it is getting toward evening."

Cleopas interrupted as he persuaded, "And the day is now nearly over."

The patient man gazed upon our pathetic faces. I recall I once stumbled upon a stray puppy that most certainly possessed the same expression as ours at that moment. "Very well, very well, upon your urging, I will stay with you," he agreed.

"You must allow us to bless you," Cleopas added, "You have shown us so much; you have shown *me* so much. I feel so foolish. How could I have ever doubted?"

With Cleopas leading the way, we walked the short distance and came upon his humble home. Cleopas quickly touched the *mezuzah* upon the doorpost and drew his fingers to his lips before entering; I followed in like manner as Cleopas continued chattering. As we entered the small home single file, we glanced behind us and noticed the man with his fingertips lingering upon the *mezuzah*, his eyes closed as if in prayer. Slowly and thoughtfully, he drew his fingers to his lips, kissed them, then opened his eyes, and entered the home. Cleopas and I, feeling quite ashamed for our casual entrance, glanced toward each other and then downward.

In the cramped room we stood upon a tightly packed dirt floor, as our traveling companion queried, "Cleopas, didn't John the Immerser struggle, just as you did, with a desire for confirmation of Yeshua's identity?"

Cleopas was attentive to the man's words but still managed to light the oil lamps, which illuminated the rocky walls within. As he began to prepare the table for a humble meal, his movements seemed more nervous. He clumsily placed the common bowl upon a low table.

I stood silent; I suppose I should have helped with the preparation, but I had never seen Cleopas this flustered as he moved swiftly about the room.

The man continued, unmoved by Cleopas's hurried activity, as he asked, "Do you remember that when John was imprisoned he sent his disciples to ask Yeshua, 'Are you the Expected One, or shall we look for someone else?'"

"I do!" I snapped. Cleopas just nodded swiftly. I then began helping Cleopas as I wondered why the man would bring up such an awkward occasion.

After cleansing our hands in the basin, we reclined at the small table as the man asked, "Was Yeshua angry with John, who felt he needed this confirmation?"

"No," Cleopas said with tremendous relief in his voice. "In fact, Yeshua answered and said to them, 'Go and report to John what you hear and see: the blind receive sight and the lame walk, the lepers are cleansed and the deaf hear, the dead are raised up, and the poor have the good news preached to them.'"

The man then interjected, finishing Cleopas's quote of Yeshua, "And blessed is he who does not take offense at me."[73]

"Quite right! That is what he said," Cleopas confirmed, knowing now that it was indeed acceptable to confirm one's beliefs with evidence to dispel one's doubts. Especially if we are to love God with all heart, soul, and *mind*.

The stranger then took the *matzah*, and with both hands upon it as he lifted it, the sleeves from his linen shirt fell slightly. For the first time we noticed a fresh, yet unusual scar upon each of his wrists. We marveled. Still lifting the *matzah* he prayed, "Blessed are You, ADONAI, our God, King of the universe, who brings forth bread from the earth."

He then broke it, stretched his arms out, handing each of us a piece, and as our fingers touched the *matzah*, we looked upon his confident, smiling face and suddenly felt the blood drain from our own. As if seeing for the first time, Cleopas and I gasped in unison as we recognized the stranger! Why, this was no *stranger* at all! It was, without a shadow of a doubt, our beloved Yeshua. It was, indeed, he who opened our minds on the road to Emmaus and who now broke bread with us! But before we could speak a word to him, as if we could even utter one, he simply vanished from our sight.[74] Once again, with our mouths agape, we were rendered, for the moment, speechless.

Suddenly I could see: my mind could see, my heart could see, and yes, my very soul could see! I could see him throughout our history. Yeshua as the one who walked with Adam and Eve, and the one who met with Abraham as Sarah laughed at the thought of having a son in their old age. Yeshua, who stayed and allowed Abraham to indulge him with his concerns as the two angels journeyed to Sodom. Yes, it was he who wrestled with Jacob and set his hip out of joint, the very one who spoke to Moses at the burning bush. Yeshua, the *I AM*, who encouraged Joshua, who stood in Nebuchadnezzar's fiery furnace with Hananiah, Mishael, and Azariah. I could see him in the Tabernacle. I could see in the Passover. I could see him as first fruits of the resurrection. And as Cleopas declared, "Because he is risen to eternal life, we will also rise to eternal life in him." As if Counting the Omer, which for me is actually a recounting of everything that God has done for his people, suddenly it all came to life. Yes, I could see—Yeshua, the *Lamb of God who takes away the sin of the world!*

We breathed hard, then slowly looked at one another, and said in unison as if reading each other's mind, "Were not our hearts burning within us while he was speaking to us on the road, while he was explaining the Scriptures to us?"

Cleopas, in one spontaneous movement, shifted to his knees upon the dirt floor and with tears streaming down his face, his arms outstretched to the sky, he loudly proclaimed the words of Isaiah the prophet, "'Behold, this is our God for whom we have waited that he might save us. This is the LORD for whom we have waited; let us rejoice and be glad in his salvation.'"[75]

I threw my head back in joyful laughter and agreement. I then grabbed Cleopas by the arm, and though it took some doing, I lifted him to his feet as quickly as I could. "Cleopas," I said, "do you know what we must do?"

"Yes, yes, my friend," he replied with breathless excitement as he tried to gather his thoughts. "We must go back to Jerusalem to tell the others he has risen indeed!"

We ran out of Cleopas's humble home and through the countryside to the bustling plateau that held Jerusalem and the home that contained the upper room where we celebrated, just days before, the *seder* with Yeshua our Lord. We knew the *talmidim* had planned to gather there this evening, and we hoped they would still be there upon our arrival. We hurried down the dusty road; our feet could not move swiftly enough. Even though we realized that, it being evening, the gates of Jerusalem would soon be closed. We also knew we could reach our destination in enough time. We had to.

We exchanged with each other, along the way, parts of the conversation that had so enlightened us. We shared our astonishment and thoughts with each other regarding that moment when our eyes were opened. We had never moved so swiftly along this road we had traveled so often back and forth to Jerusalem—to where it all began.

Now, almost twilight, we bolted back through a large stone gate of the city. I began to outrun Cleopas as we maneuvered through the city down the roads, kicking up dust and rocks, ignoring those who thought it quite unseemly that a man of Cleopas's stature should be running and shouting through the streets, "Wait for me, my friend!"

I fell upon the doorpost of our destination, breathing hard. I could feel the *mezuzah* under my fingers. I then kissed my fingertips as my mind considered the words written upon the scroll. *Sh'ma!* (Hear!) Somehow the words on that scroll were so much more meaningful to me. Everything about my faith became alive.

I could hear Cleopas's heavy footsteps and breathing behind me, and I quickly slid out of his way as he, too, fell upon the *mezuzah*, as if it had stopped his fall. His expression changed as he stretched out his arms, his hands on either side of it. He too gazed upon the *mezuzah* in a most tender way as he attempted to catch his breath. He touched it gently, thoughtfully, then slowly kissed his fingertips, and placed his hand upon his pounding heart. Then, glancing over to me, his eyes welled with meaningful tears as he commanded, "It's time to tell the others, my friend." I nodded, smiling widely.

Cleopas and I then made our way up the narrow stone staircase two steps at a time and burst into the upper room, to the place where the women had originally told us of the empty tomb. As we stood there ready to share our amazing encounter, to our astonishment, the eleven and those who were with them surrounded us saying, "The Lord has really risen and has appeared to Simon!" We then began to relate our experiences on the road to them and how we recognized him upon the breaking of the *matzah*.

Then suddenly, while we were telling these things, we saw a figure in the room out of the corner of our eyes. Yes, Yeshua himself stood in our midst and said to us, in that casual tone of his, "*Shalom alechem*," ("Peace be to you"). We were terrified. Although it is quite embarrassing to admit, I tell you truly we all just stood there startled and frightened. Indeed, we thought we were seeing a spirit.

Then he stepped toward us and said, "Why are you troubled and why do doubts arise in your hearts? See my hands and my feet, that it is I myself; touch me and see, for a spirit does not have flesh and bones as you see that I have." And when he had said this, he showed us his hands and his feet.

We looked and touched him. It was Yeshua, himself! Not a ghost, not a spirit, not our imagination, not our mind playing tricks on us but, indeed, flesh and bone. We all stood there speechless; our joy and amazement overwhelmed our senses.

Then he smiled that tender smile of his as he said those words so humorously familiar to us, "Have you anything here to eat?" That was it. It *was* him. How great of him to calm our fears and doubts by bringing us to that place of familiarity. We then reclined together and gave him a piece of a broiled fish, and right before our eyes he took it and ate it.

Then, upon leaving the place where we were, he said, "These are my words, which I spoke to you while I was still with you, that all things which are written about me in the Law of Moses and the Prophets and the Psalms must be fulfilled."

Then he opened our minds to understand the Scriptures, and he said to us, "Thus it is written, that the Messiah would suffer and rise again from the dead the third day, and that repentance for forgiveness of sins would be proclaimed in his name to all the nations, beginning from Jerusalem. You are witnesses of these things. And behold, I am sending forth the promise of my Father upon you; but you are to stay in the city until you are clothed with power from on high."

He then led us out as far as Bethany, lifted up his hands, and blessed us. Then while he was blessing us, he parted from us and was carried up into heaven. Oh, how we worshipped him there. Afterward, we returned to Jerusalem with great joy and were continually in the Temple praising God.[76]

Final Reflections

As I conclude my account of this incredible day, I am overwhelmed with the implications of what these events mean for my life. Indeed my mourning turned to joy and gladness; joy and gladness to power and purpose, which compels me to go forth, as Yeshua has called all who believe in him, to proclaim the good news of *repentance for the forgiveness of sins* and eternal life with him.

And so it is our great need—repentance. Though difficult to admit, I must acknowledge it is true. Our condition is so plain from the Scriptures. "For all of us have become like one who is unclean, and all our righteous deeds are like a filthy garment; and all of us wither like a leaf, and our iniquities, like the wind, take us away."[77]

Indeed our sins take us far away from God. Oftentimes, our reasoning causes us to believe that if we can simply offer up to him good deeds, we can then somehow attempt to make our soul right before him, yet all the good deeds in the world can never atone for our sin.

Frustrated, we then cry out to him wondering why he will not answer because the Scriptures state that it is not that he *cannot* hear us but that he *will not* as Isaiah said, "Behold, the LORD'S hand is not so short that it cannot save; nor is his ear so dull that it cannot hear. *But your iniquities have made a separation between you and your God, and your sins have hidden his face from you so that he does not hear.*[78] There is no one who calls on your name, who arouses himself to take hold of you; for *you have hidden your face from us and have delivered us into the power of our iniquities.*"[79]

Our sins—the ones we commit outwardly, those things we neglect to do according to his will, and those indulgences of the mind—are that which cause him to hide his face, his precious face, the source of blessing, from us. We are indeed, by our own choosing, delivered into the power of our iniquities.

However, to those who respond to the truth of his

word and with his stripes are healed, in Yeshua alone find their hope, purpose, joy, peace, and power. Through his sacrificial death, all may come, forsaking sin to embrace what he has done in shedding his blood to atone for the sin of the world. Just as he told Nicodemus, "For God so loved the world, that he gave his only begotten Son, that whoever believes in him shall not perish, but have eternal life. For God did not send the Son into the world to judge the world, but that the world might be saved through him. He who believes in him is not judged; he who does not believe has been judged already, because he has not believed in the name of the only begotten Son of God."[80]

Therefore, by the words of the prophet Isaiah, I implore anyone who happens upon this journal recounting the extraordinary day when my dear friend, Cleopas, and I had our eyes opened, "Seek the LORD while he may be found; call upon him while he is near. Let the wicked forsake his way and the unrighteous man his thoughts; and let him return to the LORD, and he will have compassion on him, and to our God, for he will abundantly pardon."[81]

Endnotes

1—The Encounter

[1]   John 14:1
[2]   Lev. 23:9-14
[3]   Lev. 23:15-21
[4]   1 Sam. 9:2
[5]   Isa. 53:2
[6]   Luke 24:17 (CJB)
[7]   Luke 24:18 (CJB)
[8]   Luke 24:19 (CJB)
[9]   Luke 24:19-24
[10] Luke 24:25–26
[11] Isa. 1:18a

2—The Messiah Would Be King

[12] Luke 19:38 (CJB)
[13] Zech. 9:9
[14] John 13:4
[15] 2 Sam. 7:12-13
[16] 2 Sam. 7:10-11
[17] Gen. 49:10 (NIV)
[18] Isa. 9:6
[19] Gen. 3:15

3—The Messiah Would Be Rejected and Betrayed

20   Ps. 41:9
21   Matt. 27:3-7
22   Zech. 11:12–13
23   For more information on the trial errors, see Dee Wampler's, *The Trial of Christ: A Criminal Lawyer Defends Jesus* (Springfield, MO: Self Published, 1999).
24   Ps. 27:12, 35:19-21
25   Isa. 53:7
26   Ps. 69:4
27   John 12:42-43
28   Isa. 6:10 (NIV)

4—The Messiah Would Suffer

29   John 7:25
30   Mark 3:21 (NIV)
31   1 Sam. 17:28
32   Mark 6:4
33   Ps. 69:6-8
34   John 4:31-34
35   Zech. 13:7
36   Ps. 38:10-11

5— How the Messiah Would Suffer

27   Isa. 52:14
38   Matt. 26:65–68 (CJB)
39   Please see *A Case for Christ* by Lee Strobel (Grand Rapids, MI: Zondervan Publishing House, 1998). Chapter 11 *Medical Evidence.*
40   Isa. 50:6–7
41   John 10:17–18
42   John 19:23–24
43   Matt. 27:34–44
44   Luke 23:39–43
45   Luke 23:34
46   John 19:28–34
47   Matt. 27:57–60
48   Ps. 22
49   Ps. 69:20–21
50   Isa. 53:9

6—Why the Messiah Would Suffer

51   Heb. 9:22 (CJB)
52   Lev. 17:11 (CJB)
53   John 1:29
54   Isa. 53:7
55   Isa. 52:13–53:12
56   Ps. 34:20

7— The Messiah's Resurrection

57   John 8:58
58   Num. 21:6–9
59   John 3.14–18
60   Isa. 42:6–7
61   Isa. 49:6
62   Ps. 118:22–24
63   Matt. 15:21–28
64   Matt. 8:5–11
65   Zech. 12:10
66   John 14:2–3
67   John 10:17–18
68   Ps. 16:8–10
69   John 2:19
70   Matt. 12:40
71   Luke 18:31–33
72   1 Cor. 15:20

8 — The Messiah Opened Our Eyes

73   Matt. 11:2–6
74   Luke 24:31
75   Isa. 25:9
76   Luke 24:33–53

FINAL REFLECTIONS

77   Isa. 64:6
78   Isa. 59:1–2 *(emphasis mine)*
79   Isa. 64:7
80   John 3:16–18
81   Isa. 55:6–7

About the Author

Judy Salisbury is an author, speaker, trainer, and the Founder of Logos Presentations; a multifaceted organization dedicated to helping believers live and share the Faith more effectively through various materials and speaking venues. Judy is also a home-schooling mom who volunteers with her local fire department as an E.M.T. and firefighter. The Salisbury's live on the outskirts of Mount Saint Helens in Washington State.

For more information on Judy Salisbury or the work of Logos Presentations please visit:

www.JudySalisbury.com

Personal Notes

Personal Notes

Personal Notes

Personal Notes